FISHING SKILLS

Trout Fishing

Tony Whieldon

Introduction by Russ Symons

BLANDFORD

A Blandford Book

This edition first published in the UK
1993 by Blandford, a Cassell imprint
Villiers House, 41/47 Strand, London, WC2N 5JE

Copyright © 1993 Blandford & Tony Whieldon

All rights reserved. No part of this book
may be reproduced or transmitted
in any form or by any means, electronic
or mechanical, including
photocopying, recording or any information
storage and retrieval system,
without prior permission in writing from the
copyright holder and publisher.

Distributed in the United States
by Sterling Publishing Co., Inc.
387 Park Avenue South, New York, NY 10016-8810

Distributed in Australia
by Capricorn Link (Australia) Pty Ltd
P.O. Box 665, Lane Cove, NSW 2066

British Library Cataloguing-in-Publication Data
A catalogue record for this book is available from
the British Library.

ISBN 0-7137-2386-6

Printed and bound in Great Britain by
The Bath Press, Avon.

Contents

Acknowledgments
My thanks to Michael, Graham and Bob, whose invaluable
assistance made the marathon a little shorter.

Introduction

Fly fishing for trout is rightly regarded as the most subtle of the angling disciplines, and during the last two decades it has enjoyed a tremendous growth in popularity.

In the 1960s, a government decree mandated the water authorities to open their storage reservoirs to the public, thus greatly increasing the availability of good-quality trout fishing. From that moment, the boom in trout fishing gained momentum, and today it has become a highly valued recreational activity among many of this country's three million anglers. Indeed, increasing numbers of coarse and sea anglers gravitate to the reservoirs at the beginning of each season, to add fly fishing to their repertoire of fishing skills, and to have a change from their usual sport.

Whether you are a complete newcomer to fishing, or an experienced angler, it is essential, if you are to be a successful fly fisherman, that you are able to cast properly. In addition, a good casting style will enable you to fish with precision throughout a long day without becoming tired.

It is all too easy to fall into the trap of spending a lot of money on tackle before learning to cast. This can be a complete waste, and can set back your casting ability, and therefore your success rate, for years.

Your first rod can influence your style of casting for life. If a bad habit once becomes established, it will develop into a subconscious reflex. Before you know it, you will have a flaw in your technique which may take yards off the distance at which you are able to present a fly. And all the time, you remain blissfully unaware that this is happening.

In order to cast properly, you must be using the rod that is best suited to you, and the best place to get advice on casting and tackle is at one of the many professional casting schools that now exist. No matter how well intentioned your friend is when he offers to teach you, go to a good casting school as early on as you can, and certainly before you splash out hard cash on tackle. See what the professional is using, ask his advice, try the different rods he will have available; this is all part of what you are paying for.

Carbon fibre rods have now become so cheap that when you do buy a rod, you would be well advised to go straight to this space-age material. The rod should preferably be over 9 ft (2.75 m) in length. It is more difficult to cast a short rod than a longer one, so don't buy a shorter rod in the mistaken belief that it will be easier to use. But in any event, and it bears repeating, go to a professional school and get some advice.

There is another important point about tackle that I should like to make, and it concerns fly lines. Hard-won, practical experience has proved that your choice of fly line makes all the difference between a blank day and a full bag.

A good-quality line matched to the casting power of your rod is vital to good casting. However, it is the way in which that line behaves in the water that will determine whether or not you catch your quota of fish. And before anyone gets the wrong idea, the most expensive line, in my opinion, is not always the best.

You should walk the bank of your local reservoir or river, observing what tackle the majority of fishermen are using. Is it a floating line or one that sinks? What colour line is most used? Have a natter with anglers who are resting. However, don't, whatever you do, interrupt someone who may be chasing a fish. Most anglers are polite, but in such circumstances you may suffer some verbal indignities. Ask the angler what number line he thinks is best, what make, what rod is he using, and so on. It is also a good idea to join the local angling club, as you can then ask other members for advice. When anglers have been sufficiently 'lubricated' you can learn a lot from them; in addition, you will probably be treated to many entertaining half-truths that have been stretched further than they have any right to be.

Another advantage to joining a club is that during the winter months it will probably run a fly-tying class. Your local adult education centre may also run one, and it is well worth the effort to attend. Not only will tying your own flies save you money, but also the experience of landing a good fish on a fly which you have tied yourself is one of the most satisfying aspects of fly fishing. At first you will be tempted to try your hand at all sorts of wonderfully fluffy, highly-coloured lures, but over the years it is the simple, easily-tied flies which have endured and caught fish for generations of fly fishermen.

Make sure, when you step forth onto the bank for the first time, that your fly wallet is well stocked with classically simple flies, such as the legendary Black and Peacock spider, stick fly, worm fly, sedge pupa, and a few simply-tied lures, such as the Sweeny Todd, Black lure and Appetiser. These will be sufficient to catch fish under most conditions. Indeed a few of the very best fly fishermen rarely use more than half a dozen patterns right through the season, and catch just as many fish as any of us: a classic example of the rule which applies to all forms of fishing, 'Keep it simple and straightforward'.

When the author, Tony Whieldon, asked me to write this introduction to his book, I was both honoured and a little horrified at the task, because I know him to be a very able fly fisherman. What he has done in this book, as well as to demonstrate his superb draughtsmanship, is to show you his down-to-earth grasp of the information you need to know to catch trout, and I know he will join with me in wishing you 'Tight Lines'.

Russ Symons,
Plymouth, Devon.

Rods

Most fly rods are manufactured from carbon fibre although some in the budget price range are still made with fibreglass. Lengths vary between 7ft (2·15m) and 11ft (3·30m). Very short wand-like rods are ideal for use with lightweight lines on streams and small stillwater fisheries. Longer models are used with heavier lines on larger rivers or for distance casting from the bank on stillwaters. Some very long rods are also made to take medium-weight lines and used for traditional short-line loch fishing from a drifting boat. The line rating is clearly marked, just above the handle, with the letters AFTM followed by the recommended line size. For example, a rod marked AFTM 6/7 would perform at its best with a № 6 or a № 7 line.

Line guides on fly rods are either the snake variety or single leg lined, with always a lined tip and butt guide.

Snake

Single Leg Lined

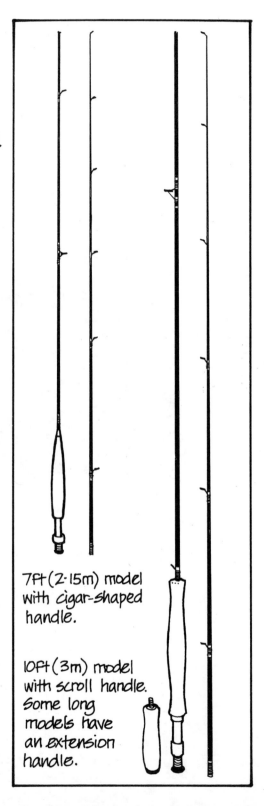

7ft (2·15m) model with cigar-shaped handle.

10ft (3m) model with scroll handle. Some long models have an extension handle.

Reels

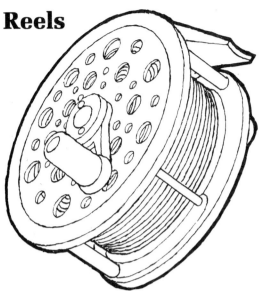

Wide drum multiplier reel with line and backing for use with the 9ft 6in(2·90m) rod.

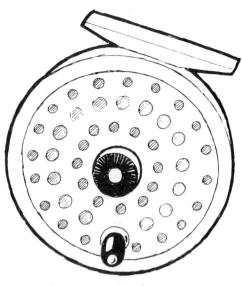

Lightweight magnesium, single action reel holding a 4-5 line, for use with the 7ft(2·15m) carbon rod.

Standard drum, single action reel holding 5-7 double taper floating line for use with the 11ft (3·35m) loch-style rod.

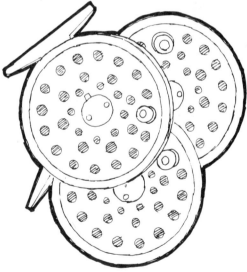

A selection of lines loaded on to spare spools or reels will be needed for the 9ft6in (2·90m) rod. eg., WF Floater, WF Sinker, or Shooting Head Floater and Sinker and DT Floater.

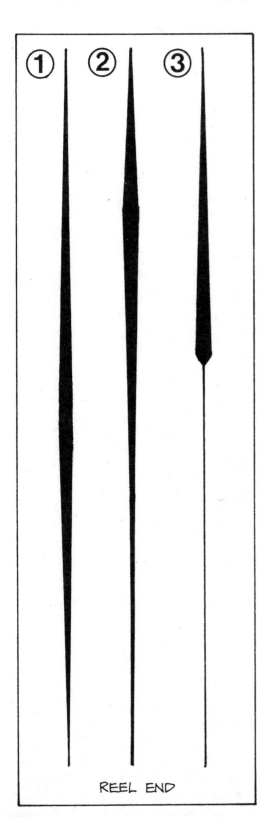

REEL END

Lines

① DOUBLE TAPER

The standard length for a fly line is 30yd (27·43m). For delicate presentation for close to medium-distance casting the DT is ideal. The economical advantage of this line is that it can be reversed, as each end is a mirror image of the other.

② WEIGHT FORWARD

Longer casts can be produced with this line, but with the drawback that when the line alights on the water surface quite a disturbance is created.

③ SHOOTING HEAD

This consists of what is virtually a double-taper line cut in half with an ample supply of much finer backing or shooting line tied to the rear end. It is capable of producing very long-distance casts.

Lines

The profiles shown previously can all be obtained in different densities — here they are.

FLOATING
For dry fly and traditional loch-style fishing — when the trout are feeding close to the surface. It can also be used in conjunction with a weighted nymph for deeper-lying fish.

INTERMEDIATE
A very useful, extremely slow sinking line which can be retrieved at a snails pace and still present the fly at a constant depth.

SLOW SINKING
Ideal for exploring various depths in medium-depth water. Fish will often take on-the-drop, when this line is being used.

MEDIUM AND FAST SINKING
For presenting a lure close to the bottom in medium depth and very deep water. The fast sinking line is best for fishing a Booby-type nymph or lure.

Leaders

The leader is probably the most important part of the fly fisherman's armoury. It is the finest, weakest link in the chain and should, therefore, be paid constant attention. The point, or tippet, is the most vulnerable area and should be inspected regularly during the fishing session, and especially after landing a fish, for signs of abrasion caused by the fish's sharp teeth. If the tippet has been affected then renew it immediately. In any case, it is always a good policy to tie on a new tippet at the beginning of every session.

Leaders can be bought, ready-made or they can be constructed from lengths of nylon from 50m spools.

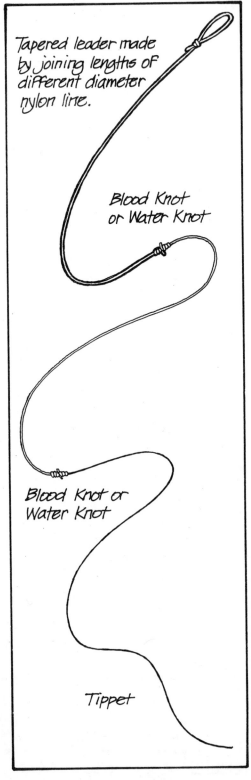

Tapered leader made by joining lengths of different diameter nylon line.

Blood Knot or Water Knot

Blood Knot or Water Knot

Tippet

Connecting line to leader

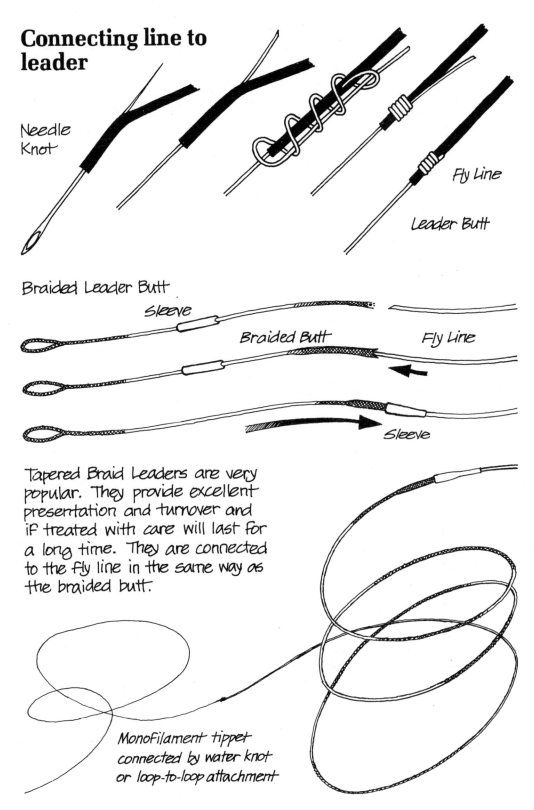

Needle
Knot

Fly Line

Leader Butt

Braided Leader Butt

Sleeve

Braided Butt

Fly Line

Sleeve

Tapered Braid Leaders are very
popular. They provide excellent
presentation and turnover and
if treated with care will last for
a long time. They are connected
to the fly line in the same way as
the braided butt.

Monofilament tippet
connected by water knot
or loop-to-loop attachment

Backing

As the overall length of a fly line is no more than 30yd (27m), it is necessary to increase the volume of line on the reel by adding several yards of backing. The amount of backing required will depend on the size of the reel. Wide-drum reels are generally used for lake fishing and obviously take more line than a standard spool, which is normally used for fishing on small to medium rivers. To find the answer, wind the fly line on to the spool, attach the backing to the line, then wind the backing on to the reel until it lies about ⅛in (3mm) beneath the housing supports. Remove the backing and line from the reel, reverse, and wind on again, backing first. Attach the backing to the spool with the knot shown below.

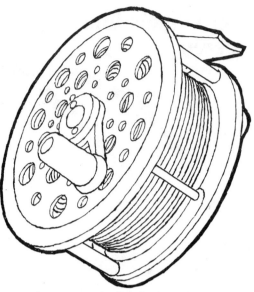

A correctly loaded reel

It is customary, when fishing still-waters, to have a selection of reels, each loaded with a different line. This will allow the angler to cope with the varied conditions and fish behaviour encountered on lakes.

When fishing on running water, a floating line is usually sufficient.

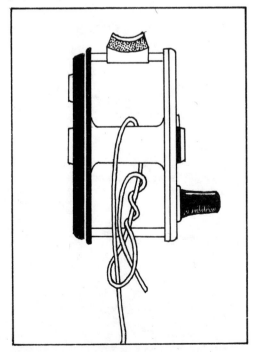

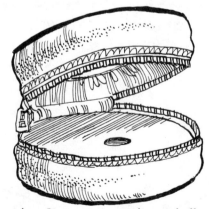

Look after your reels and they won't let you down. Reel cases keep out grit and dust which could harm the mechanism of the reel and the coating of the line.

Fly hooks

The classic fly hook, having a shape ideally suited to traditional wet fly patterns. Dry flies can also be tied on this design but it is best to use a sproat with an upturned eye for very small imitations. Before tying a fly to a new hook, always check that the eye has been formed correctly.

Sproat

Nymphs can be tied on any standard or long shank hook, but this special design with its narrow gape and slightly angled eye lends itself admirably to most nymph dressings.

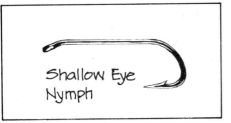

Shallow Eye Nymph

The most widely used hook for lures and streamer flies. It is also suitable for long-bodied nymph imitations such as pheasant tails and various damsel fly nymphs.

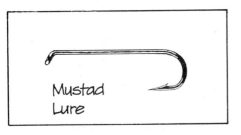

Mustad Lure

The perfect hook for sedge pupa imitations and various other nymphs, giving a very life-like appearance. It can also be used to give the curved swimming atitude of the freshwater shrimp.

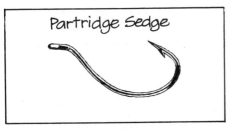

Partridge Sedge

SPROAT

MUSTAD LURE

SHALLOW EYE NYMPH

PARTRIDGE SEDGE

Artificial flies

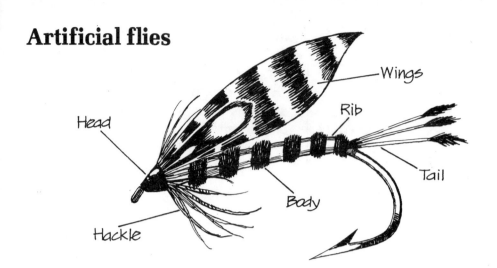

Wings

Rib

Head

Tail

Body

Hackle

DRY FLIES

Used when fish are taking insects from the surface. Equally effective on river and lake. Most dry flies are tied with the purpose of imitating, as closely as possible, a particular species of insect.

WET FLIES

Some of the traditional wet fly patterns bear some resemblance to aquatic life, but on the whole they are bright and flashy. The smaller, hackled wet flies used by the river angler for upstream fishing are, on the other hand, most life-like.

LURES

These probably account for more stillwater trout than all the other types combined, mainly because of their more widespread use. Colours used in their construction are as varied as the spectrum. They represent small fish rather than aquatic insect life.

NYMPHS

Mostly fished in conjunction with a floating line. Some patterns are weighted by the inclusion of lead wire beneath the body material. Of all the artificials, these are the most life-like. Patterns vary from the very small buzzer pupae up to the large damselfly nymphs.

Mayflies

These artificials represent the largest of the British mayflies, *Ephemera danica*, which appears on rivers and lakes during May, June or July.

Fan-winged Mayfly

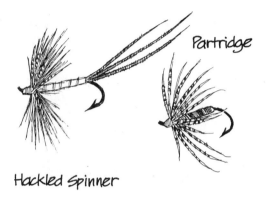

Partridge

Hackled Spinner

Hackle-point Spent Spinner

Popper lure

Anything less like a fly is hard to imagine, but this cork headed creation can be cast well enough with orthodox fly gear, and accounts for many good trout.

Use in conjunction with a floating line and retrieve with long steady pulls, across the water surface.

Dry flies

Black Gnat

Hawthorn

Hares Ear

Grey Duster

Knotted Midge

Alder

Coch-y-Bonddu

Baigent's Black

Walker's Sedge

G and H Sedge

Greenwell's Glory

Pheasant Tail

Daddy Longlegs

Coachman

Iron Blue Dun

Blue Upright

Dark Varient

Wickham's Fancy

Red Spinner

Silver Sedge

Wet flies

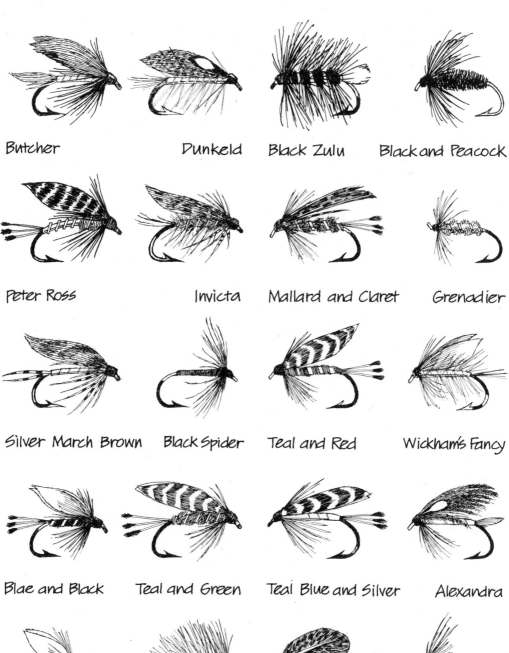

Butcher

Dunkeld

Black Zulu

Black and Peacock

Peter Ross

Invicta

Mallard and Claret

Grenadier

Silver March Brown

Black Spider

Teal and Red

Wickham's Fancy

Blae and Black

Teal and Green

Teal Blue and Silver

Alexandra

Coachman

Red Palmer

Parson Hughes

Black Pennell

Lures

Ace of Spades

Appetizer

Missionary

Jack Frost

Muddler Minnow

Church Fry

Baby Doll

Polystickle

Sweeny Todd

Whisky Fly

Lures

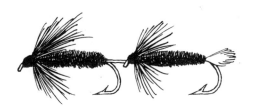

Worm Fly

Black and Orange Marabou

Badger Lure

Black Lure

Dog Nobbler

Jersey Herd

Perch Fry

Undertaker

Matuka

Elver Lure

Nymphs

Amber Nymphs

Mayfly Nymph

Damselfly Nymph

Pheasant Tail Nymph

Damsel Wiggle Nymph

Stick Fly

Collyer's Nymph

Montana Stone

Persuader

Brown Caddis

Nymphs and pupae

Midge Pupae

Footballer

Leaded Shrimp

Chompers

Corixa

Corixa (Plastazote)

Longhorns

Iven's Nymph

PVC Nymph

Sedge Pupae

Sawyer's Pheasant Tail Nymph

Bloodworm

Silver Nymph

Alder Larva

Cove's Pheasant Tail

Casting a fly

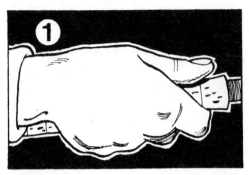

Hold the rod with the thumb on top of the handle.

Hold the line between the handle and the butt ring.

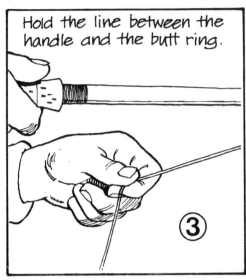

③

Pull enough line from the reel to reach the required distance.

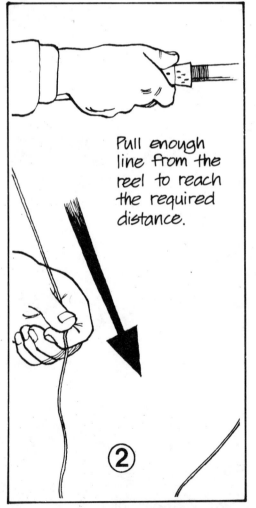

②

Lift the rod quickly but smoothly, and at the same time pull on the line.

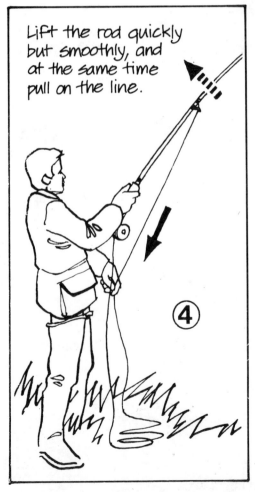

④

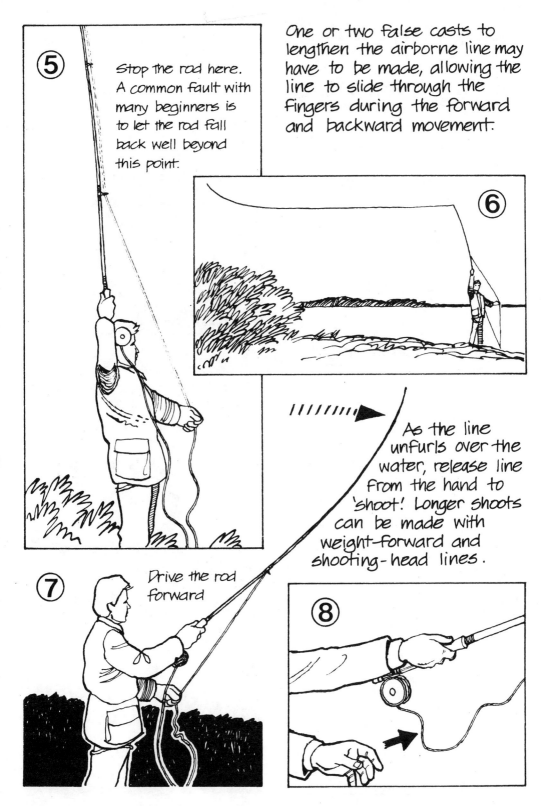

⑤ Stop the rod here. A common fault with many beginners is to let the rod fall back well beyond this point.

One or two false casts to lengthen the airborne line may have to be made, allowing the line to slide through the fingers during the forward and backward movement.

⑥

As the line unfurls over the water, release line from the hand to 'shoot'. Longer shoots can be made with weight-forward and shooting-head lines.

⑦ Drive the rod forward

⑧

Fishing a floating line

When the fish are active up in the surface area, and especially if you can see insects being blown on to the water surface, and being taken by the fish, it is worth using a dry fly.

Before the fly is cast, it should be 'dunked' in a bottle of floatant.

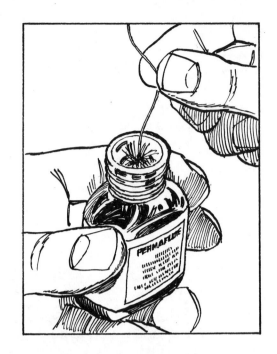

Dragging the fly across the surface in short erratic jerks will often produce a response.

A floating line can also be used to fish a nymph on or very near the bottom. In this case the leader will have to be longer than usual, (15ft (4·55m), and the nymph will need a weighted body (leaded nymph).

Whenever nymphs are being used, it is advisable to give the leader a wipe with 'leader sink'; a good substitute is washing-up liquid.

Fishing a floating line

Sometimes a trout will be seen leaving a trail of rings as it cruises just beneath the surface, sucking down insects which lie in its path. By logical deduction, it is possible to place your offering accurately ahead of the fish.

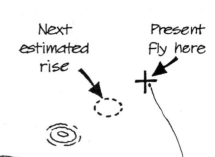

Next estimated rise

Present fly here

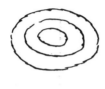

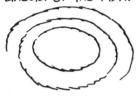

As nymphs or pupae rise to the surface to hatch, they are often intercepted by the fish before they reach the surface. This activity is perceptible only to the keenest eye. Binoculars are a great help when trout are feeding like this.

After the cast, pause awhile to let your nymph sink well beneath the surface, then retrieve line very slowly, pausing occasionally to keep the nymph about 12 in (30 cm) under the surface film.

Fishing a sinking line

Of the different types of sinking line the very slow sinker is the most versatile. It can be used to overcome a cross-wind problem, or to fish a nymph or lure in the upper layers of water, or over weedbeds and underwater snags.

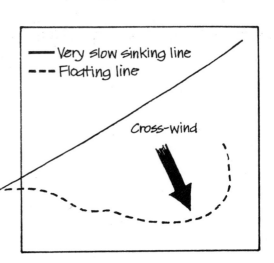

— Very slow sinking line
--- Floating line

Cross-wind

A positive way to locate fish with any form of sinking line is to use the count-down process.

First cast—count to 10 seconds, then retrieve line.

Second cast—count to 15 seconds, then retrieve line.

Third cast—count to 20 seconds, then retrieve line, and so on.

When trout are located, continue to fish at the same counting depth.

The way to retrieve a lure

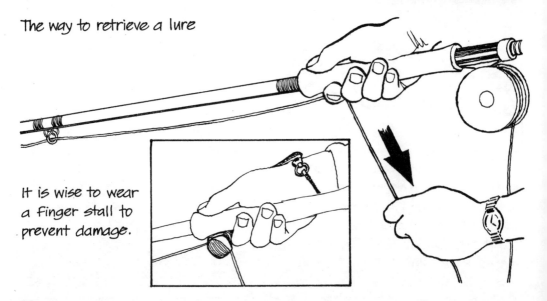

It is wise to wear a finger stall to prevent damage.

Although the very slow-sinking line is versatile it would not be practical to use it exclusively, as it would take far too long to sink to fish that were lying well down in very deep water.

When searching for fish in these deeper places use a fast, or very fast sinking line.

Fishing a sinking line

When retrieving a lure, especially quickly, it is important to hold the rod correctly in relation to the line. Some trout will take a lure in a very savage manner. It is therefore best to hold the rod at an angle to the line, in order to cushion the shock of a taking trout.

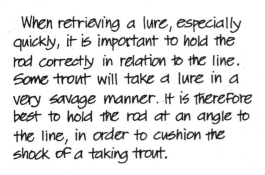

WRONG

CORRECT

Species of trout

BROWN TROUT

RAINBOW TROUT

BROOK TROUT

Brown trout (Salmo trutta fario) are indigenous to the British Isles and Europe.

Rainbow trout (Salmo gairdneri) were introduced to Britain and Europe in the 1880s and are used extensively to stock stillwater fisheries.

American brook trout (Salvelinus fontinalis) is a char, introduced from North America, which can be cross-bred with both brown and rainbow trout. A brook/brown trout cross is known as a 'tiger trout.'

Cannibal trout

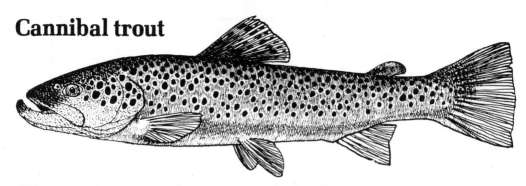

After reaching a certain size, all brown trout will readily consume small fish as well as insects, but some resort to a diet consisting wholly of fish — trout included. River browns that adopt this life style seldom, if ever, rise to take flies from the surface but lie well down in the deeper pools. The one exception which may rouse them from their fish-eating habit is a very heavy hatch of the large mayfly, *Ephemera danica*. If the food supply is sparse, a river cannibal can be a sorry sight with a large head and long, thin body.

In the large lakes of Scotland, Ireland and Wales these trout are called *Ferox*. Because of the rich pickings in such waters, most of these stillwater cannibals are really good-looking creatures. Some anglers fish for them with deeply-sunk lures, trailed behind a boat. Occasionally these trout are taken on the fly, more especially during a hatch of *danica* or after dark when they tend to move nearer the surface.

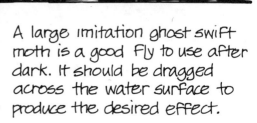

A large imitation ghost swift moth is a good fly to use after dark. It should be dragged across the water surface to produce the desired effect.

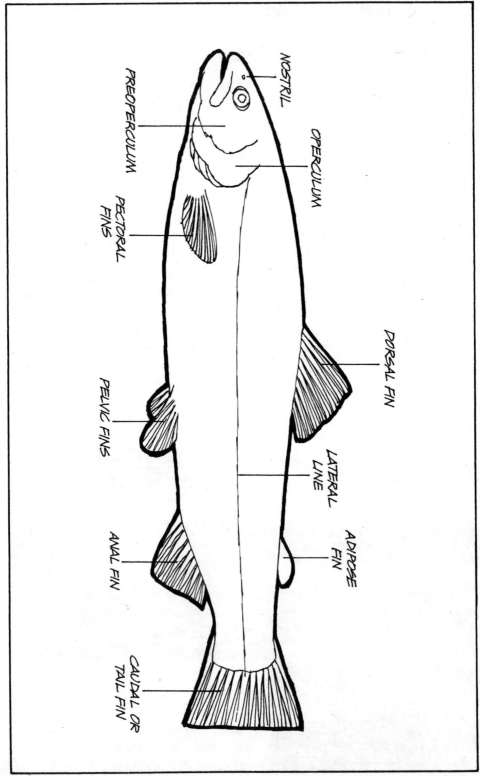

NOSTRIL

PREOPERCULUM

OPERCULUM

PECTORAL FINS

DORSAL FIN

PELVIC FINS

LATERAL LINE

ADIPOSE FIN

ANAL FIN

CAUDAL OR TAIL FIN

The trout's diet

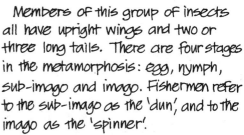

Members of this group of insects all have upright wings and two or three long tails. There are four stages in the metamorphosis: egg, nymph, sub-imago and imago. Fishermen refer to the sub-imago as the 'dun', and to the imago as the 'spinner'.

At the surface the 'dun' emerges from the nymphal skin.

The 'spinner' then emerges from the 'dun'.

After mating, the eggs are deposited into the water, and both male and female fall to the water surface as 'spent spinners'.

Nymphs are also taken by trout as they swim towards the surface.

These dead and dying flies are easy prey for trout.

After hatching from the egg the nymph lives and feeds on the bottom. Some are eaten at this stage by foraging trout.

The trout's diet

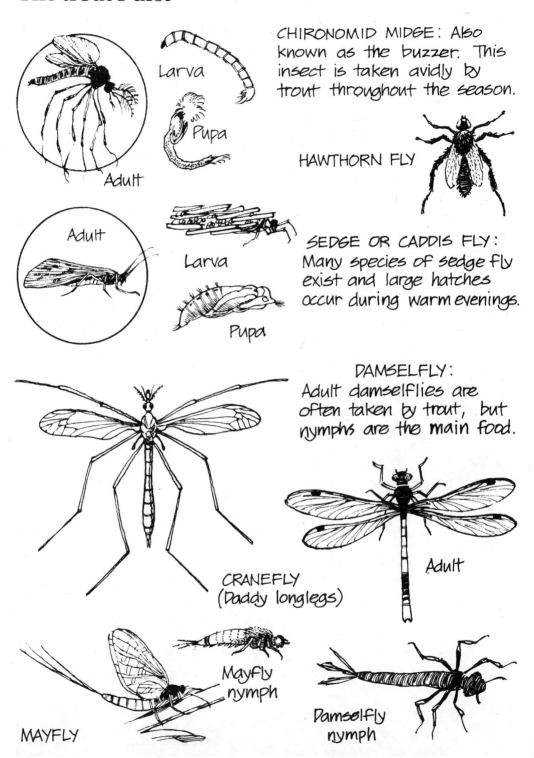

CHIRONOMID MIDGE: Also known as the buzzer. This insect is taken avidly by trout throughout the season.

Larva

Pupa

Adult

HAWTHORN FLY

Adult

Larva

Pupa

SEDGE OR CADDIS FLY: Many species of sedge fly exist and large hatches occur during warm evenings.

DAMSELFLY: Adult damselflies are often taken by trout, but nymphs are the main food.

CRANEFLY (Daddy longlegs)

Adult

Mayfly nymph

MAYFLY

Damselfly nymph

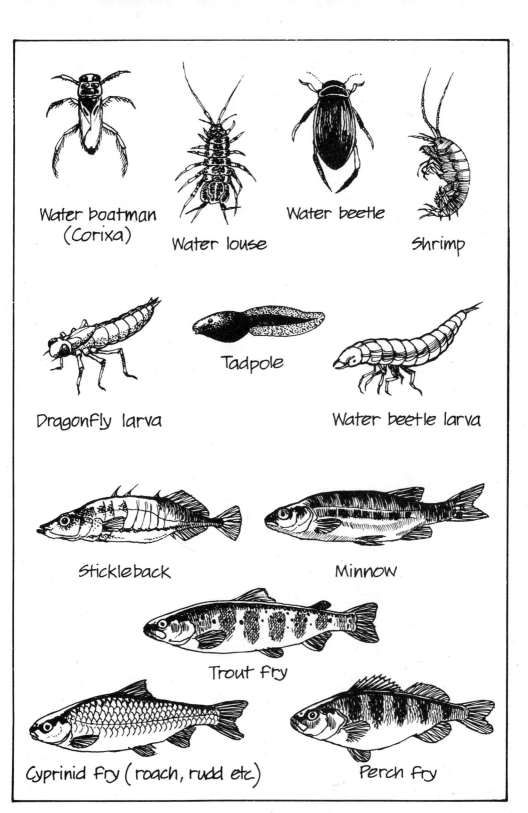

Water boatman (Corixa)

Water louse

Water beetle

Shrimp

Dragonfly larva

Tadpole

Water beetle larva

Stickleback

Minnow

Trout fry

Cyprinid fry (roach, rudd etc.)

Perch fry

Fishing a midge pupa

This artificial is meant to represent the pupae of chironomidae (midges) which hang in the surface film before their final metamorphosis into the adult midge (buzzer).

To ensure that the artificial hangs stationary in the surface film, the leader should be greased so that it floats. Mount two or three on the leader, each one stopped by a blood knot. Tie a sedge, well treated with floatant, on the point to act as an additional buoy.

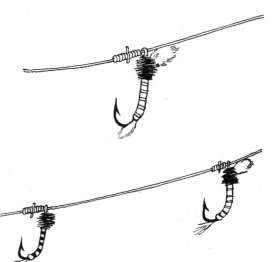

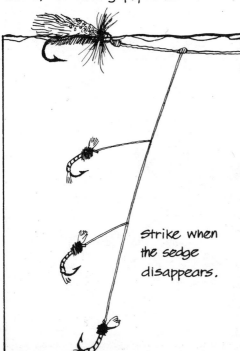

Set-up for fishing pupae near the bottom.

Strike when the sedge disappears.

Midge pupae can also be fished in the traditional style, and retrieved very slowly.

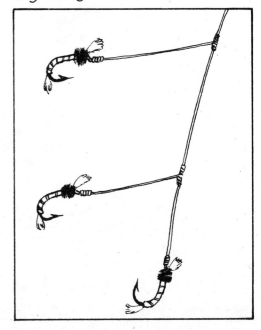

Fishing a sedge pupa

This pattern is a general representation of the many different sedge pupae found in most stillwaters. During the summer months, the natural swims to the surface, or to the shore, in order to undergo the final transformation and become an adult sedge fly.

The artificial can be fished at mid-water, or near the bottom with a sinking line ....

.... or just under the surface with a floating, sink-tip, or very slow-sinking line.

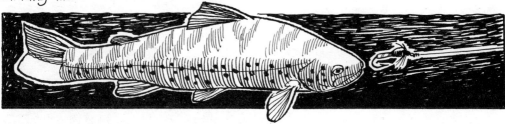

Retrieve the pupa at a medium pace, with long steady pulls, and a pause here and there.

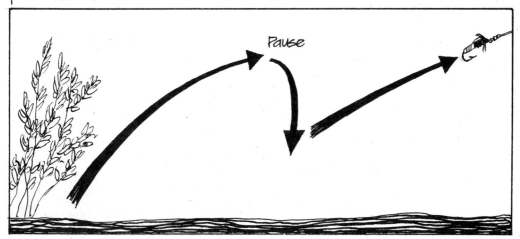

Pause

Fishing a damselfly nymph

During the early part of the season this pattern can be fished, very slowly, along the bottom. Shallower bays, where weed is prolific during the summer, are the most likely areas to attract the natural nymphs, as they feed largely on decaying vegetable matter.

During the warmer months the nymphs are far more active and wriggle to the surface, whereupon they proceed to swim towards the shore or surface weed in order to hatch into adult damselflies. To simulate this activity, fish the artificial just under the surface with a fairly fast retrieve, on a floating line.

Where there are rushes or reeds, it is often more productive to cast and retrieve along the shoreline.

Fishing a daddy-long-legs

The crane fly or 'daddy-long-legs' is a familiar sight at the water-side from June onwards. They are often blown onto the water surface where they struggle in their attempts to become air-borne once more. Such a large insect presents a good mouthful to the trout, which respond avidly.

Cast the artificial to an area where trout activity is obvious on the surface, (the fly will need to be well 'dunked' in floatant), then just wait for a fish to find it.

When a take does occur, resist the temptation to strike, as the trout will often try to drown the fly first, before taking it in its mouth.

Wait until the line starts to run out, then lift the rod high to set the hook.

Drag a 'daddy-long-legs' through a heavy ripple, or waves, and the trout will often respond with a very positive take.

Fishing a corixa

This pattern imitates the lesser water-boatman which spends most of its life near the bed of the lake, but has to rise to the surface in order to replenish its air supply.

Two patterns have developed to represent this little bug. The leaded version, which can be fished via a floating or a sinking line close to the bottom...

... and the buoyant (plastazote) version, which has to be fished with a sinking line.

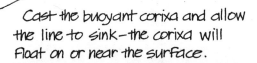

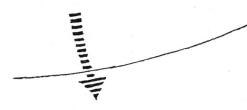

Cast the buoyant corixa and allow the line to sink—the corixa will float on or near the surface.

When the line is retrieved, the corixa will dive towards the bottom, imitating, in a very life-like manner, the action of a water-boatman as it swims back to base.

40

Fishing a leaded shrimp

This pattern represents the fresh-water shrimp, Gammarus; a resident of well-oxygenated water. They thrive in watercress, suggesting therefore that lakes fed by streams containing this plant would be ideal places to use this very effective little pattern.

The combination of lead wire and the shape of the body results in the artificial adopting an inverted attitude, which simulates the natural in a very life-like manner.

A leaded shrimp is ideally suited for margin fishing in clear-water lakes. Let the shrimp sink to the bottom where trout are patrolling.

When a trout approaches, inch the shrimp off the bottom in short jerks.

Lake fishing

MOUNTAIN LAKE
Contains native wild trout which are usually small, but there are exceptions where the average size is good.

RESERVOIR
Man-made lake, created by damming the course of a stream. Found in mountainous and lowland areas. Most reservoirs are regularly stocked with trout by the water authorities.

PRIVATE FISHERY
Usually created by excavation and fed by spring or stream. Regularly stocked with large trout.

LOWLAND LAKE
The best examples of this type of lake are the limestone loughs of Ireland. Contains resident wild brown trout which grow to a very large size.

Lake fishing from the bank

Always use the longest rod you can handle for fishing large lakes and reservoirs. A weight forward line will certainly make casting easier if there is a wind blowing, but if the water surface is smooth or only slightly rippled, a double taper line which falls lightly on the water will result in more takes.

A long leader may present problems in a wind, producing 'wind knots', but it is always worth using a leader at least the same length as the rod, especially in clear water.

A long-handled landing net is far more suitable for lake fishing than the short, folding variety used for river fishing.

Wading is often necessary to cover feeding fish on lakes with a very gently sloping shore line, but there are restrictions on wading in some waters, so it is best to check before doing so. Always be prepared for the weather on large, exposed lakes by taking a waterproof jacket and overtrousers.

Lake fishing from the bank

When fish are showing on the surface, they are usually feeding on
insects which have been blown on to
the water surface from the shore,
or on nymphs or pupae hanging in
the surface film.

If there are a number of fish
rising fairly close together, cast
among them and work the fly back
slowly in very short jerks.

Method of retrieving a small fly or
or nymph with a floating line.

ing the wind

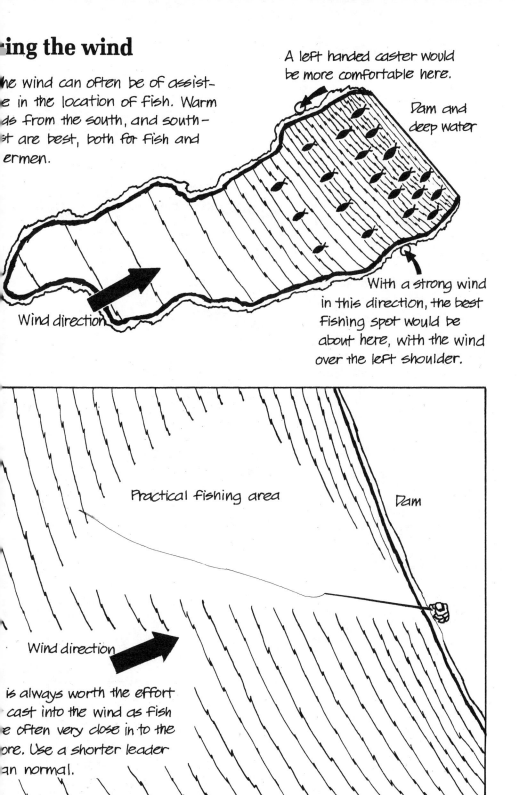

he wind can often be of assist-
e in the location of fish. Warm
ds from the south, and south-
st are best, both for fish and
ermen.

A left handed caster would
be more comfortable here.

Dam and
deep water

Wind direction

With a strong wind
in this direction, the best
fishing spot would be
about here, with the wind
over the left shoulder.

Practical fishing area

Dam

Wind direction

is always worth the effort
cast into the wind as fish
e often very close in to the
ore. Use a shorter leader
an normal.

Fishing a lure from the bank

Hungry, early-season trout will grab almost any lure that is cast into a lake. Some lakes at this time of year tend to carry a certain amount of colour, which demands the use of a high-visibility lure, such as a Jack Frost, Appetizer, Ace of Spades or Dog Nobbler.

As the season advances, however, the food supply is more abundant, and the trout become more selective. Nymphs and flies are then the main items of food, but where fish fry exist these are also taken, and it is possible to imitate them with a lure. The shallows of many lakes support a healthy population of sticklebacks, minnows and other small fry on which the trout feed.

High visibility lures

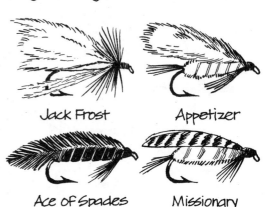

Jack Frost   Appetizer

Ace of Spades   Missionary

Fry imitators

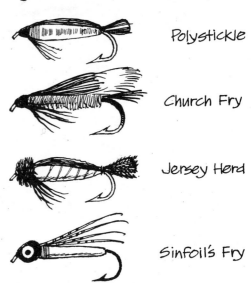

Polystickle

Church Fry

Jersey Herd

Sinfoil's Fry

Where fry activity is seen, cast a fry lure along the shore-line.

Fishing a lure from the bank

The Dog Nobbler is rather unusual inasmuch as it carries a whole split-shot as part of its dressing. It certainly does not represent anything in particular, but when drawn through the water it has a very stimulating action.

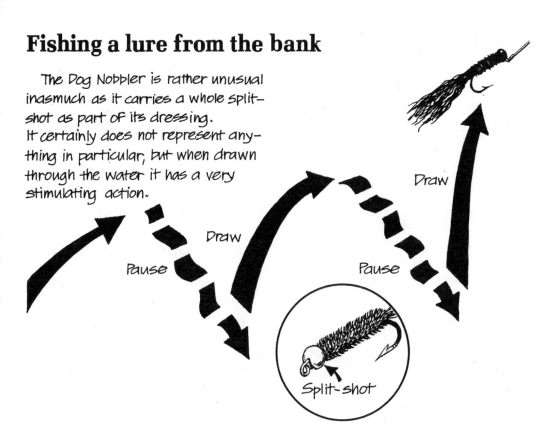

Draw

Pause

Draw

Pause

Split-shot

Another unique lure is the Muddler Minnow, which has the tendency to float, rather than sink like the Dog Nobbler. In medium-depth water it works better on a floating line; but in deep water, a slow-sinking line is more suitable if the fish are swimming deeper.

Loch-style

This popular, traditional method is performed by repeatedly casting a short line and a team of wet flies ahead of a drifting boat. May is an ideal month to start loch-style fishing, especially if the hawthorn fly is on the water.

WIND ➡

①

DRIFT ➡

① Using an 11ft (3·35m) rod, cast a double-taper floating line, with a rating of 4-7, two rod lengths ahead of the boat.
② When the flies are in the water, lift the rod through an arc from A to B, thus imparting a smooth, continual retrieve to the flies. Keeping in touch with the flies by pulling line with the free hand may also be necessary.
③ Flick the line back and repeat the process.

POSITION AT POINT B

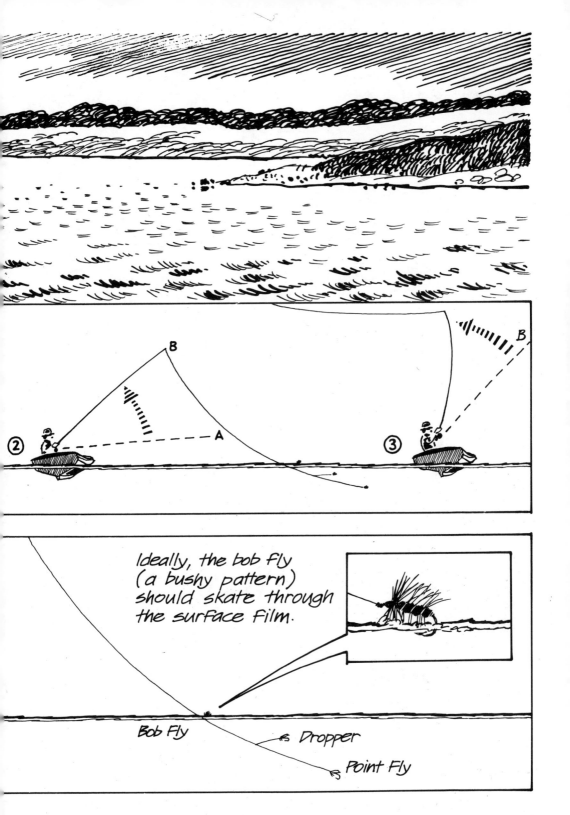

② B A

③ B

Ideally, the bob fly (a bushy pattern) should skate through the surface film.

Bob Fly

Dropper

Point Fly

Lake fishing from a boat

Casting a dry fly to rising trout is a delightful form of boat-fishing.

This is particularly effective when flies, especially hawthorn flies and crane flies, are being blown on to the lake from the shore.

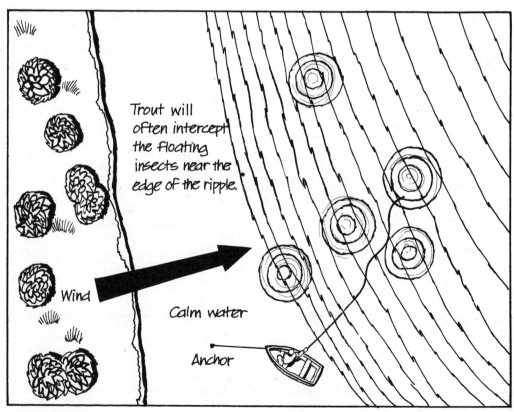

Trout will often intercept the floating insects near the edge of the ripple.

Wind

Calm water

Anchor

Dapping with a daddy-long-legs

Dapping with a natural daddy-long-legs has been a method of angling practised for many years, on some Irish and Scottish lochs.

Given the right conditions, this form of fishing can be applied to most stillwater fisheries. There is no need to use the natural insect either—an artificial 'daddy' works just as well.

The boat is allowed to drift before the wind, just as with the loch-style of wet fly fishing. The rod, however, needs to be as long as possible in order to present plenty of line to the wind.

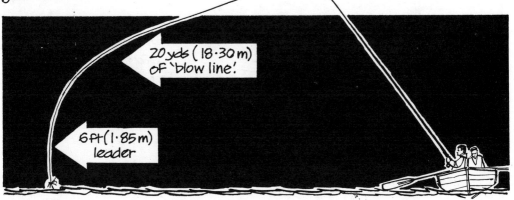

20 yds (18·30 m) of 'blow line'

6 ft (1·85 m) leader

Simply let the line blow out over the water, and attempt to keep the fly dancing in the waves.

With this method, an over-hasty strike will result in a missed fish. Wait until the trout has turned down with the fly in its mouth, then just tighten up.

Lure fishing from a boat is undoubtedly a very productive form of trout fishing. A single lure can be fished just beneath the surface, at mid-water, or on the bottom.

Lure fishing from a boat

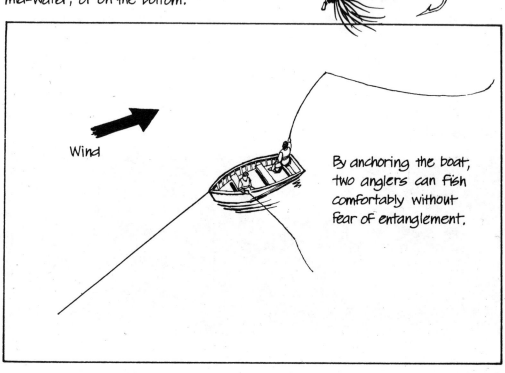

Wind

By anchoring the boat, two anglers can fish comfortably without fear of entanglement.

Expect a take at any time, even when the retrieve has almost finished. Some really vicious takes occur when the lure is close under the boat.

Trolling

This method involves trailing a lure about 30-40 yd (28-36 m) behind a boat. A lead core line is used to keep the lure well down in the water. Large, tandem hook lures are the most effective.

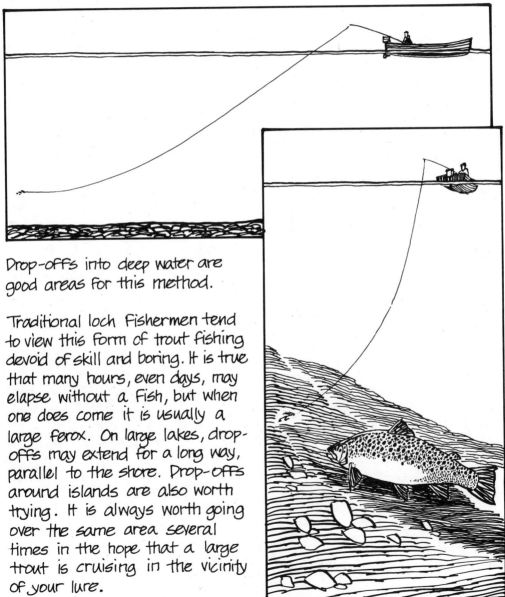

Drop-offs into deep water are good areas for this method.

Traditional loch fishermen tend to view this form of trout fishing devoid of skill and boring. It is true that many hours, even days, may elapse without a fish, but when one does come it is usually a large ferox. On large lakes, drop-offs may extend for a long way, parallel to the shore. Drop-offs around islands are also worth trying. It is always worth going over the same area several times in the hope that a large trout is cruising in the vicinity of your lure.

River and stream fishing

Trout can be found in most rivers and streams where the water is clean. The trout of the fast rocky streams of the higher ground are usually small in comparison to the fish of the lowland rivers. Because of the turbulent nature of the rocky stream, wet fly fishing is the method most widely employed. On the lowland river, where the flow is more sedate, the dry fly is favoured.

— Moorland stream

Lowland stream

River and stream fishing

There is no need for a heavy line when fishing a stream. No's. 4,5 or 6 will be ideal. A light coloured line will show up far better in the shadows of overhanging foliage.

Other items needed will include; waders, strong tackle bag with a wide shoulder strap, collapsible landing net, priest, fly floatant, leader sink (if nymph fishing), scissors, spare leaders and a selection of flies.

River and stream fishing

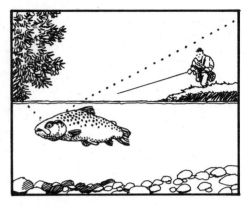

A stealthy approach is the key to success when fishing on rivers, especially smaller ones. Tread very lightly to avoid sending vibrations through the water and keep a low profile, out of the trout's field of vision.

Never stand on a high bank, against the sky, when casting to a trout. This will be like a red warning flag to the fish and send it bolting for cover.

It is always best to keep as close to the water line as possible and in summer, when the water level is low, this may well mean having to kneel in the water if you are casting to a trout which is rising at the tail of a pool.

Wear drab-coloured clothing to blend in well with the bankside foliage. An olive green ex-army combat jacket is ideal for this.

Wading is often necessary on streams with dense bankside foliage. This should be done slowly, with great care and only through shallow areas. Sand is the ideal bottom material on which to wade — pebbles are noisy and send vibrations in all directions.

On banks with sparse growth, take advantage of every bit of cover in order to avoid spooking a rising trout.

Fly presentation

When fishing in the confines of an overgrown stream the overhead cast is seldom practical. Instead, use the side cast.

The principal and timing of the side cast are the same as those of the overhead cast.

Pause

Work the line on an imaginary plane between overhanging foliage and the water surface.

When fishing a dry fly, wet fly or nymph directly upstream, or across and up, the angler has to recover line at the speed of the current in order to maintain contact with the fly.

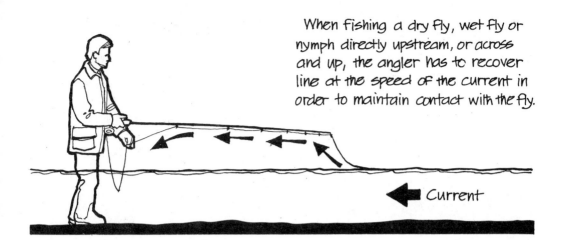

Current

When fishing from the bank on a small stream, with a short line on the water, the same effect can be achieved by moving the rod.

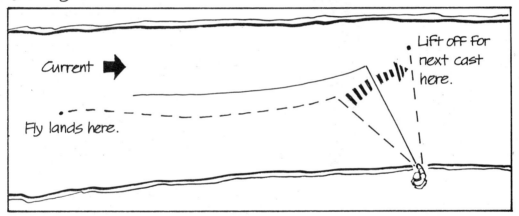

Current

Fly lands here.

Lift off for next cast here.

Presentation of a floating fly directly downstream.

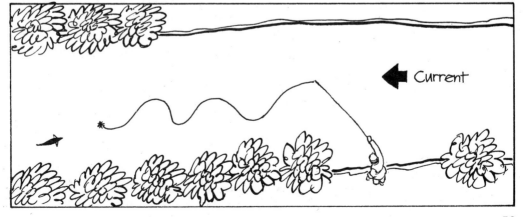

Current

Trout in a river always lie with their heads facing upstream, so it therefore makes sense to approach them from the rear, gradually working your way upstream.

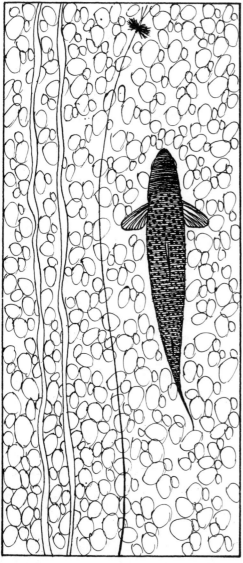

A correctly-presented fly should alight, gently, just ahead of the rising trout. If the fly lands too far ahead of the trout, the line may fall into the trout's field of vision.

Dry fly presentation

When you have to fish across the stream to the trout, you should have no problem as long as the flow is even from bank to bank.

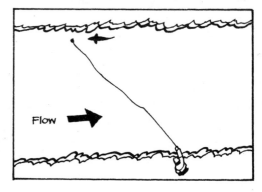

Flow ➡

Unfortunately, conditions do not always present a perfect situation.

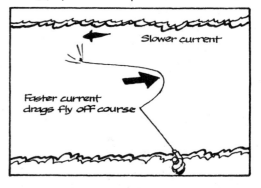

Slower current

Faster current drags fly off course

The remedy for this is to create some slack line.

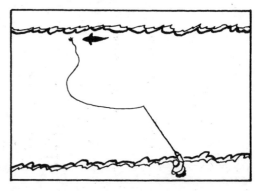

Dry fly presentation

When two or more trout are rising in close proximity to one another, care must be taken to select the fish in the correct order, to avoid scaring the other fish.

There are occasions when rises are few and far between, but this does not mean efforts with the dry fly will prove fruitless. Cover every likely-looking spot with a cast or two, and be prepared for a take just as if you had cast to a rising fish. Here are some places worth trying.

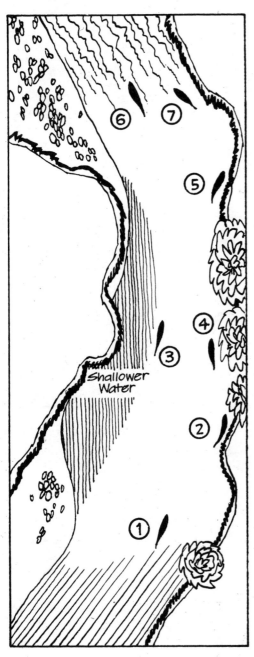

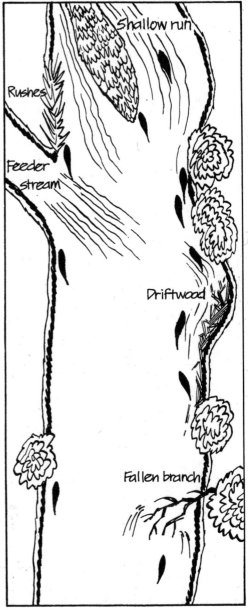

Upstream wet fly

Smaller, fast-flowing, overgrown streams are ideally suited to the upstream wet fly method.

Trout lies in a small rocky river

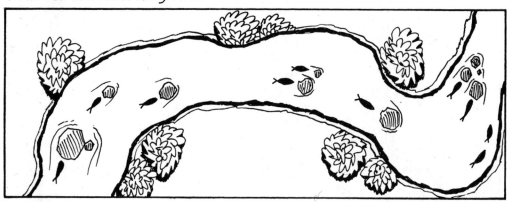

The angler inches his way upstream casting his flies, on a short line, into every likely-looking spot.

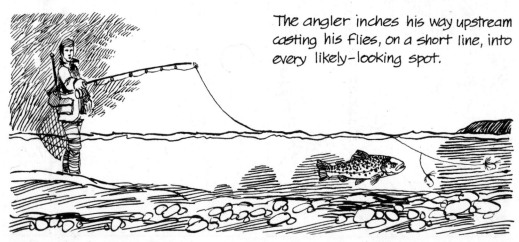

The downstream method

This method is practised with a team of, usually, three flies, similar to that used in the traditional loch method, but using smaller patterns. It is best employed on the larger, swiftly-flowing rocky rivers.

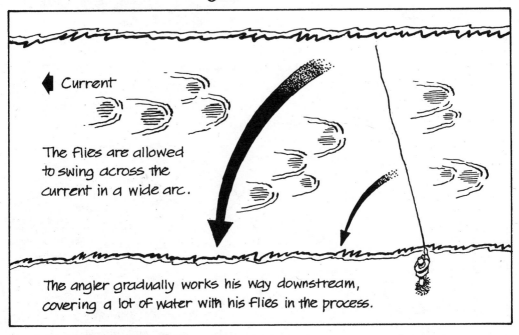

◀ Current

The flies are allowed to swing across the current in a wide arc.

The angler gradually works his way downstream, covering a lot of water with his flies in the process.

Pay special attention to the quieter water on the downstream side of large stones.

The more sedate flow of the low-land river is ideally suited to fishing a nymph. Nymph fishing comes into its own when the trout are not feeding on the imago, but are intercepting the nymph as it swims to the surface or is being carried along in the flow of the current. If trout are 'bulging' just beneath the surface, or are showing their tails, then this is the time to tie on a nymph.

Presenting a nymph in running water

The artificial nymph is fished singly and cast upstream; in fact, the whole procedure is like dry fly fishing, except that here the nymph is meant to sink as soon as it hits the water. In nymph fishing, the avoidance of drag is not important. Nymphs are free-swimming and the trout take them as they swim in all directions.

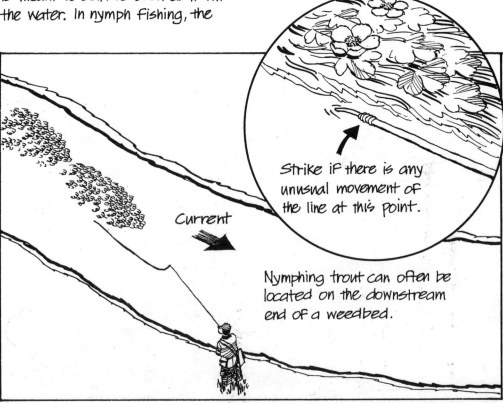

Current

Strike if there is any unusual movement of the line at this point.

Nymphing trout can often be located on the downstream end of a weedbed.

Small stream dapping

On many small streams bank-side foliage is so dense as to make ortho-dox fly presentation impossible. How-ever, the angler who uses a little init-iative and stealth, can extract trout that would make the locals gasp with astonishment.

The angler should walk slowly and quietly along the bank, or sit in a position which affords a reasonable view of the water. Eventually a trout will show itself by rising.

The angler should then take up a position directly over the fish. Conceal-ment and stealth are now even more important. The rod is poked through the foliage and the fly lowered until it touches the surface of the water. Some movement can be imparted to the fly by jiggling the rod-tip.

When the trout takes the fly, the rod-tip should be lowered before lifting into the fish.

A long-handled net is almost always necessary to extract trout from these confined places.

Ideal patterns for stream dapping.

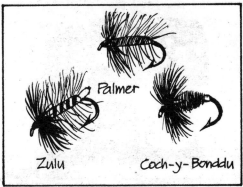

Palmer

Zulu   Coch-y-Bonddu

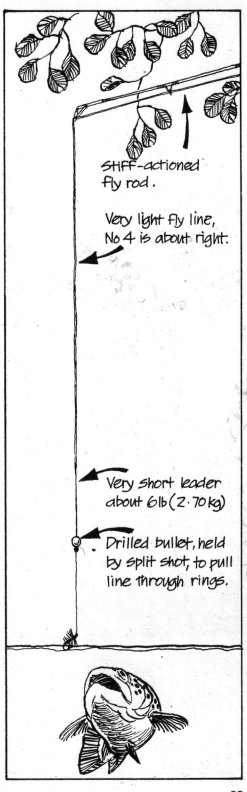

Stiff-actioned fly rod.

Very light fly line, No 4 is about right.

Very short leader about 6lb (2.70 kg)

Drilled bullet, held by split shot, to pull line through rings.

Playing and landing

1

As soon as a trout is hooked, hold the rod well up.

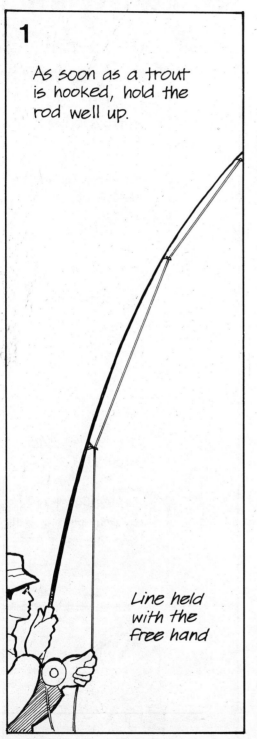

Line held with the free hand

2

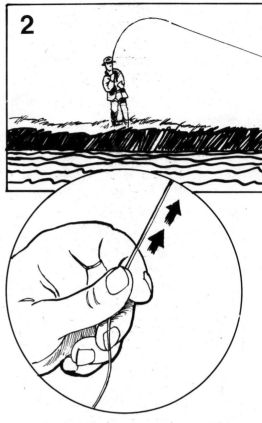

.... by letting the line slip, under pressure, through the index finger and thumb.

4

The fish can now be played from the reel.

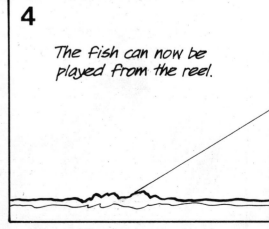

When a trout feels the resistance of the rod and line it will often take off on a powerful run, and should be given its head....

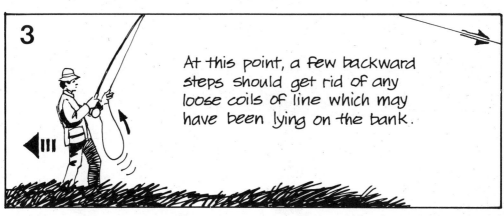

3

At this point, a few backward steps should get rid of any loose coils of line which may have been lying on the bank.

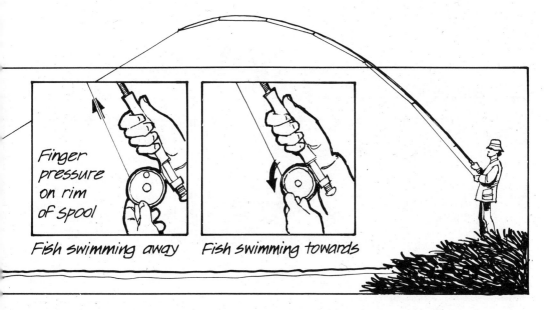

Finger pressure on rim of spool

Fish swimming away   Fish swimming towards

5

Many anglers play a fish directly from the line, and while this is fine up to a point, and very efficient for keeping in touch with a trout which is swimming rapidly towards the angler, there is the problem of having loose coils of line lying on the bank which could become snagged or tangled and result in a lost fish.

The best way to turn a trout away from snags is to apply side strain.

6

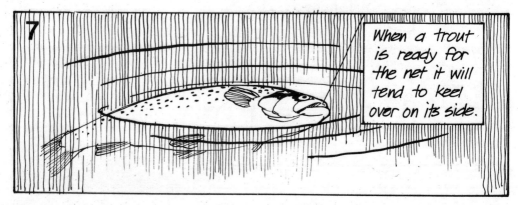

7

When a trout is ready for the net it will tend to keel over on its side.

8

9

10

11

Draw the fish over the frame of the stationary net. NEVER jab at the fish in an attempt to scoop it out.

Lift the frame clear of the water, draw the net towards the bank and lift, stepping back at the same time. The last three movements should be done in one smooth easy action. Large trout will probably have to be dragged up the bank.

Takes

A trout taking a wet fly, fished downstream in fast water, will often hook itself. The angler feels a tug and the fish is on.

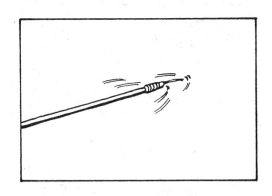

The take of a trout accepting an upstream wet fly or nymph is far more subtle. The best way to detect these takes is to watch the end of the fly line. When a take occurs the line will stop or be drawn to one side or upstream. Then is the time to tighten into the fish.

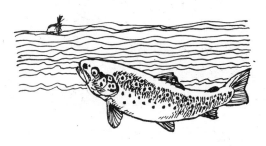

A small trout, snatching at a dry fly in a fast stream, needs to be struck very quickly with a flick of the wrist.

Larger trout in slower, quieter water should be allowed to turn well down with the fly. In fact, it is often advisable to wait until the line starts to move forward. This is particularly important on the majority of stillwaters.

Accessories

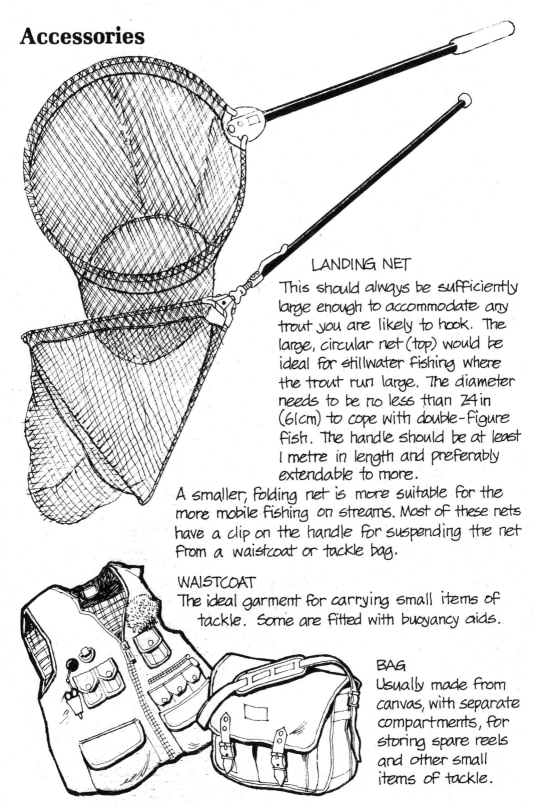

LANDING NET
This should always be sufficiently large enough to accommodate any trout you are likely to hook. The large, circular net (top) would be ideal for stillwater fishing where the trout run large. The diameter needs to be no less than 24 in (61cm) to cope with double-figure fish. The handle should be at least 1 metre in length and preferably extendable to more.

A smaller, folding net is more suitable for the more mobile fishing on streams. Most of these nets have a clip on the handle for suspending the net from a waistcoat or tackle bag.

WAISTCOAT
The ideal garment for carrying small items of tackle. Some are fitted with buoyancy aids.

BAG
Usually made from canvas, with separate compartments, for storing spare reels and other small items of tackle.

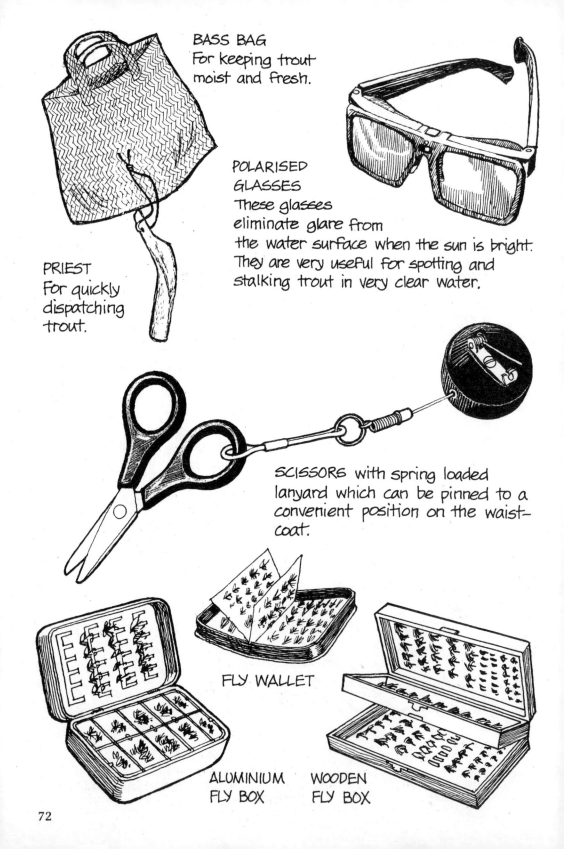

BASS BAG
For keeping trout moist and fresh.

POLARISED
GLASSES
These glasses eliminate glare from the water surface when the sun is bright. They are very useful for spotting and stalking trout in very clear water.

PRIEST
For quickly dispatching trout.

SCISSORS with spring loaded lanyard which can be pinned to a convenient position on the waist-coat.

FLY WALLET

ALUMINIUM FLY BOX

WOODEN FLY BOX

Knots

BLOOD KNOT: For joining lengths of different breaking strain nylon in order to produce a tapered leader. Recommended breaking strains are shown in another section of this book.

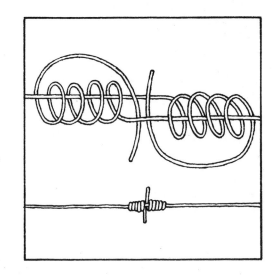

TUCKED HALF-BLOOD KNOT: Unlike the basic half-blood knot, this knot will not slip, and is the ideal knot for connecting a fly to the point or dropper of a leader.

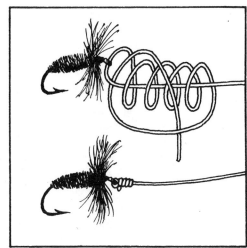

DROPPER KNOT: There is more than one knot can be used for this purpose. The water knot shown, however, permits the use of nylon equal in breaking strain to that of the point to be connected further up, where the main leader is thicker.

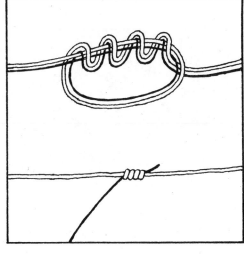

Knots

Here are three more knots which can be used to secure a fly to a leader.
These knots are more suited to small dry flies — use the tucked half blood knot for larger hooks.

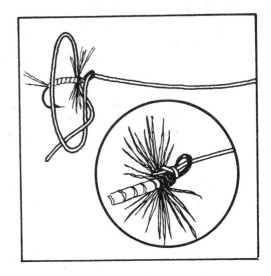

HALF HITCH

TURLE KNOT

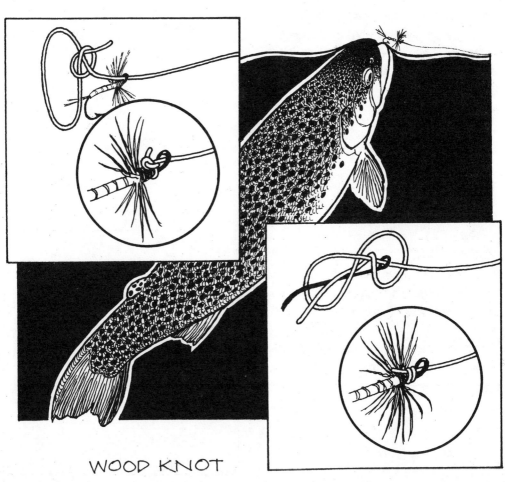

WOOD KNOT

How to cure a loose ferrule

Spigot ferrules, especially those on carbon fibre rods, tend to wear loose very quickly.

Spigot ferrule

A loose ferrule can be noticed immediately, because the male and female sections are touching one another when the rod is assembled.

To produce a tighter fit, rub the male section with candle wax.

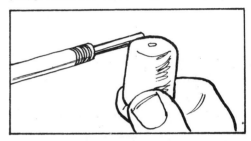

If the ferrule is very badly worn, more drastic measures will have to be taken.

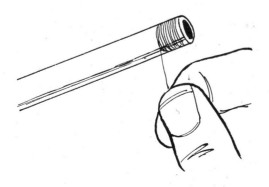

Cut about ¼ in (6 mm) from the female section, then re-whip to provide support.

A correctly fitting spigot ferrule should look like this.

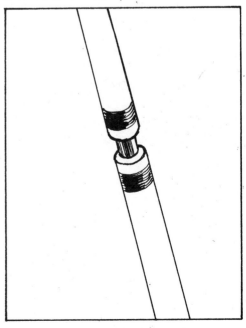

Whipping on a ring

Rods can be purchased in a half completed state, with just the handle and reel fitting secured to the blank. The rings are left to the angler. Ring positioning information is provided with the rod.

Start by securing one side of each ring to the rod. Sellotape is the ideal material for this.

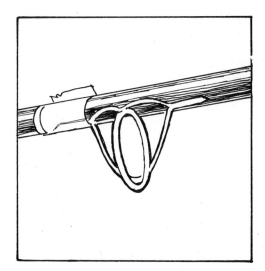

If single leg fuji rings are being used, a drop of super-glue will keep them in position, ready for whipping. Now is the time to make sure that all the rings are exactly in line.

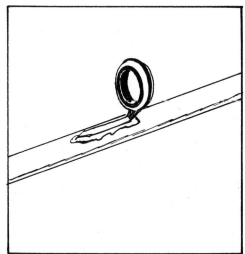

Starting at a point on the rod, just clear of the foot of the ring, wind the whipping thread back on itself for five or six turns, and cut off the tag end.

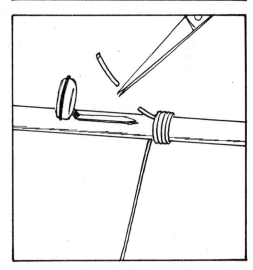

Whipping on a ring

Continue whipping, making sure that the turns are tight to one another. About five turns short of where you intend to finish, insert a loop of whipping thread or nylon monofilament, and continue whipping over this loop.

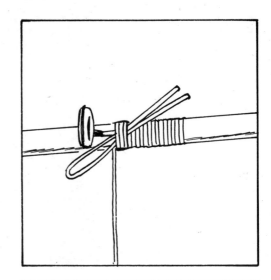

Making sure that a steady tension is being maintained, push the end of the whipping through the eye of the loop.

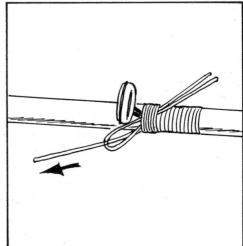

Pull the loop through the whipping, and keep pulling until the end of the whipping is completely through. Cut off the tag end.

If the ring has two feet, repeat the whole operation, after removing the sellotape. When all the rings are secured coat the whippings with two or three layers of varnish.

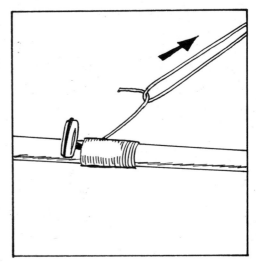

Licence

Before you go rushing off to the nearest river or lake to catch a trout, you will need to be in possession of a rod licence. This licence does not give you the right to fish without the riparian owner's consent. You may be lucky enough to know an owner who is prepared to let you fish just for the asking, but on the majority of regularly stocked trout waters, it will be necessary to purchase a permit before you can fish.

It is not uncommon, when fly fishing for trout, to catch immature salmon (parr) which should be returned to the water immediately. The one positive means of identification is to check the position of the eye in relation to the jaw, as shown in the diagram.

If you fish on a stream where salmon parr are numerous, it would be a noble gesture to flatten the hook barb so that the parr can be returned with the minimum of delay.

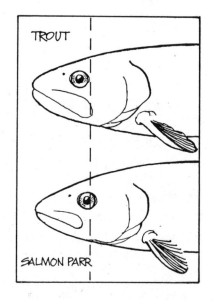

River Authority Regions

There are ten river authority regions in England and Wales which are all covered by the national rod licence. However, certain byelaws may vary from region to region so it is advisable to check before fishing an unfamiliar water.

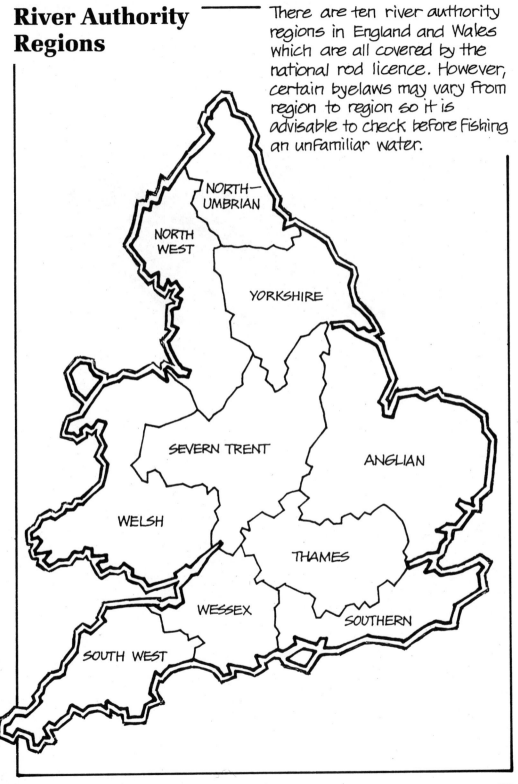